TABLE OF CONTENTS

INTRODUCTION

"In investment, it is not about timing the market; it is about time in the market. Do not wait for the 'perfect' moment- focus on the right age, which is now. Start today and let the process of compounding work for you, so you can stop trading your life for time.

The bridge between starting today and achieving true wealth is patience- a force that rewards every income group equally by allowing growth to work its magic. Ultimately, you start letting time work for you, instead of you working for time."

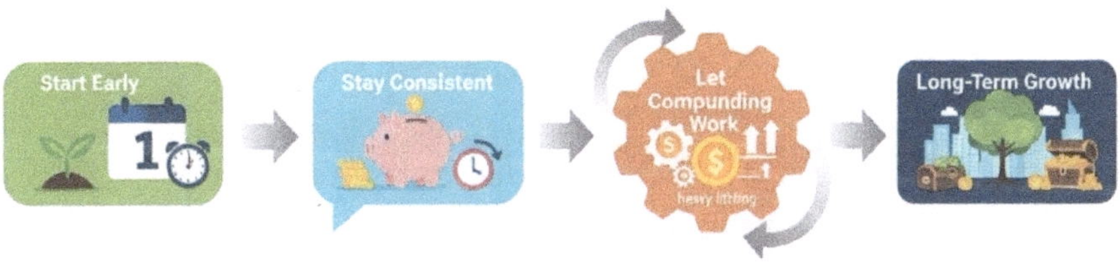

Success in the market comes from treating investment and trading as a disciplined business rather than a game of chance. By focusing on market patterns and practical systems, it becomes possible to understand how wealth is truly built and protected over time. While these insights are not provided by a SEBI-registered advisor, they are rooted in hands-on experience and a long-term approach designed to build a lasting financial foundation rather than just a temporary income.

This framework serves individuals across all financial backgrounds- whether starting with modest capital or managing an existing portfolio- to create a structured plan spanning 10 to 30 years.
The objective is to empower a mindset where compounding performs the heavy lifting. Ultimately, this approach shifts the focus from trading life for money to letting wealth grow independently.

Investment is more about habits than mathematics. Real wealth is not built through shortcuts; it is built by staying patient and making smart choices repeatedly. Many people underestimate the power of steady progress.

In the end, the winner isn't the person with the highest IQ- it's the person with the most patience and self-control.

YOUR WEALTH ROADMAP

This book is built around three realistic timelines, helping you match your money with your life goals:

- The 10-Year Plan: Building your foundation and confidence
- The 20-Year Plan: Mastering consistency and market cycles
- The 30-Year Plan: Securing your retirement and independence

Beyond the plans, one will learn about the "rules of the road":

- how long to hold your assets?
- when it actually makes sense to withdraw & how much one can withdraw keeping the investment going on?
- how to stay calm when the market gets shaky?

We keep things grounded by accounting for real-world factors like inflation, taxes, and market cycles, so your expectations remain realistic.

NAVIGATING THIS GUIDE

1. This is a manual for a long-term business, not a "get-rich-quick" story.
2. Read it slowly.
3. Reflect on your own situation and comfort level.
4. The goal is not just to finish the pages, but to apply these ideas to your own life at a pace that works for you.

History shows that your long-term results are not determined by how much money you start with, but by the habits you keep.
Many people delay investing because they are waiting for a large sum of money or "perfect" market conditions. In reality, what matters most is getting the right knowledge to clear away myths. Even small, regular contributions- when combined with patience, can grow into something significant over the years.

This book is built on realistic expectations. We factor in the "hidden" costs- inflation, taxes, and market cycles, so your plan stays grounded. The goal is to replace emotional "guessing" with a calm, business-like approach to growth.

Investing is a lifelong process, not a one-time event. You will face periods of growth and periods of uncertainty.
Success doesn't come from avoiding market storms, but from staying disciplined through them.

With this mindset, we begin our journey with, " Chapter 1: The Foundation of Investing", which lays down the essential principles that form the base of every successful long-term plan.

CHAPTER 1:
THE FOUNDATION OF INVESTING

Every long-term investment journey begins with a strong foundation. Without understanding the basics, even the best opportunities can lead to poor outcomes. Before thinking about returns, strategies, or timelines, it is essential to understand what investing truly means and how it differs from saving or speculation.

At its core, investing is the process of putting money to work over time with the expectation that it will grow through disciplined decision-making, patience, and compounding. Unlike short-term trading, long-term investing focuses on time, consistency, and risk management—not quick gains.

Many people enter the market driven by excitement, fear of missing out (FOMO), or short-term news. This often leads to frequent buying and selling, emotional decisions, and eventual disappointment. A strong foundation helps you avoid these mistakes by providing clarity, structure, and a long-term perspective.

Before moving into 10-year, 20-year, or 30-year investment plans, one must first understand three core principles:

1. Time in the market matters more than timing the market
2. Consistency beats intensity
3. Risk can be managed, but not eliminated

These principles will guide every decision discussed in this book, from portfolio construction to withdrawals and navigating market downturns.

SAVING VS INVESTING

Many people use the words "saving" and "investing" interchangeably, but they serve very different purposes. Understanding this distinction is essential before committing money for the long term.

Saving is primarily about safety and liquidity.

Money kept in savings accounts or fixed deposits is intended for short-term needs, emergencies, or planned expenses. While savings provide stability, they often struggle to grow faster than inflation over long periods.

Investing, on the other hand, is designed for growth.

It involves placing money into assets like equities or funds that have the potential to walk parallel with inflation and increase in value.

This process requires patience and emotional mastery in exchange for higher long-term returns.

The mistake many individuals make is trying to treat savings like investments or investments like savings. This confusion leads to disappointment and the premature withdrawal of funds during market fluctuations.

WHY MOST PEOPLE FAIL AT INVESTING?

Failure in the market is rarely caused by a lack of intelligence; it is more often the result of emotional decision-making. Fear during declines and greed during rallies push investors to act against their own interests.

Common reasons for failure include:

- ***Chasing short-term returns***
- ***Reacting to noise***
- ***Panic selling***
- ***Lack of a horizon***

A strong foundation helps you avoid these pitfalls. By providing clarity and structure, it prevents emotional reactions from controlling your financial future.

POWER OF COMPOUNDING

Compounding is the process through which money grows not only on the original amount invested but also on the returns it generates over time. It is often described as one of the most powerful forces in long-term investing because its impact increases significantly with time.
In the early years, the growth from compounding may appear slow and unnoticeable. *This is the "waiting period" where many investors lose patience and stop.* However, as time passes, the effect becomes stronger and growth accelerates without the need for additional effort.

What makes compounding truly effective is time, not frequent buying and selling. The longer your money remains invested, the more opportunities it has to grow on top of its own growth. This "quiet growth" in the background is what eventually separates those who achieve financial independence from those who simply save.

WHY STARTING EARLY MATTERS?

Starting early gives compounding the one thing it needs most: time. Even small, regular investments made early in life can outperform significantly larger investments made later. The difference lies not in the total amount contributed, but in how long those funds are allowed to grow.
Delaying your investment journey by even a few years can drastically reduce long-term outcomes. Once time is lost, it cannot be recovered. This is why consistency from an early stage is far more valuable than trying to catch up by investing larger amounts later in life.
The lesson is simple:
Begin early, stay consistent, & let compounding to do the heavy lifting.

- Years 1–5 (Slow): Results are small; patience is vital
- Years 6–15 (Steady): Momentum builds; growth is visible
- Years 16–30+ (Rapid): Harvest phase; growth turns exponential

"Compounding rewards patience, not urgency."

UNDERSTANDING RISK AND VOLATILITY

Risk and volatility are often misunderstood. Most "market risk" is simply short-term fluctuation, not permanent loss.

- 📉 Volatility (The "Price" of Growth): Short-term price swings caused by news, interest rates, or global events. It is a temporary and unavoidable part of the journey.
- ⚠️ Real Risk (The "Point" of Failure): True risk is not price movement; it is making decisions that permanently damage your wealth.

💡 The Lesson: Real risk is not short-term volatility. It is abandoning a well-planned strategy due to fear or exiting the market during a temporary downtrend.

WHY VOLATILITY IS NOT YOUR ENEMY?

Volatility is not just a hurdle; it is an opportunity. Market downtrend allows disciplined investors to accumulate assets at lower prices, significantly improving long-term outcomes.

A successful investment approach accepts short-term discomfort in exchange for long-term progress.

- ✅ The Reward: Those who remain calm during fluctuations are historically rewarded with higher growth.
- ❌ The Trade-off: Avoiding all volatility usually means avoiding all growth.

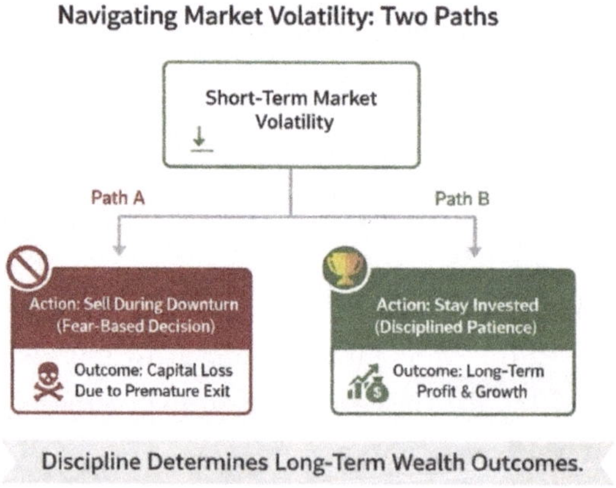

CHAPTER 2:
TIME- THE REAL DRIVER OF WEALTH CREATION

Investment outcomes are shaped less by individual decisions and more by the length of time those decisions are allowed to work. Time is not just a passive background element; it is your most powerful planning variable.

Before selecting a strategy, an instrument, or an asset allocation, you must determine your time horizon. This duration dictates:

- **Goal Capacity**: What you can realistically achieve.
- **Absorption**: How much market fluctuation your portfolio can withstand.
- **Flexibility**: Your ability to stay calm during global or economic uncertainty.

TIMELINE: THE ARCHITECT OF YOUR STRATEGY

Without a defined time horizon, investment decisions lack a foundation. Your timeline dictates your behavior:

- ***Short horizons-*** *demand caution and precision to protect capital*
- ***Long horizons-*** *allow for resilience, adjustment, and the absorption of market swings*

Many investment failures occur due to a mismatch of time.

Financial damage happens when capital intended for long-term goals is managed with short-term fear, or when short-term money is exposed to long-term volatility.

"Defining your time horizon, first simplifies decisions and later, reduces unnecessary action."

THE THREE TIME HORIZONS

Long-term investing can be broadly organized into three time horizons. These are not rigid rules or guarantees; but planning frameworks that help align expectations with reality.

INVESTMENT TIME HORIZONS- AT A GLANCE

Time Horizon	Primary Purpose	Planning Focus
10-Years	Foundation	Stability & flexibility
20-Years	Expansion	Continuity & growth
30-Years	Sustainability	Preservation & control

"These horizons reflect a strategic intent, serving as a roadmap for practical decision-making."

THE 10-YEAR HORIZON- *ESTABLISHING THE BASE*

This horizon is suitable for goals that require growth while still allowing for access and adaptability.
Because capital invested for 10-years is exposed to full market cycles- including temporary declines. The objective is not aggressive maximization, but allowing sufficient time for outcomes to stabilize.
In this window, decisions should remain limited, deliberate, and strictly aligned with the original purpose of the investment.

THE 20-YEAR HORIZON- *EXPANSION AND STABILITY*

This horizon supports larger financial goals that benefit from extended participation in economic growth. With a longer recovery window, the impact of individual market events diminishes; decision frequency naturally reduces, and outcomes become more consistent over time.

In this phase, the strategic focus shifts from reactive adjustment to compounding continuity.

THE 30-YEAR HORIZON- *LONG-TERM SUSTAINABILITY*

This horizon applies to goals that prioritize endurance and long-term financial independence. Here, the capital is structured for longevity. The risk exposure is managed thoughtfully, and withdrawals- if any, are planned rather than reactive. The objective is not constant growth, but maintaining control and sustainability across decades.

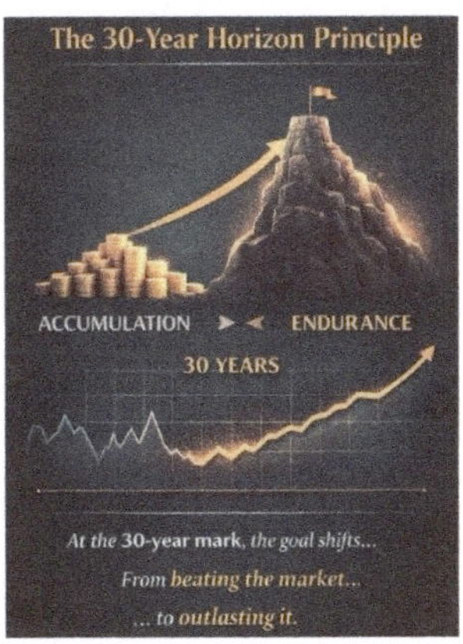

THE 10-YEAR LITMUS TEST

Many investors approach the market with an "exit target" in mind- planning to liquidate the moment a specific return is achieved.
This mindset mistakenly treats investing as a short-term transaction rather than a continuous, long-term process.
Investment functions at its peak, when capital is given the space to absorb uncertainty, recover from disruptions, and compound gradually.
To ensure this, a fundamental filter must be applied before committing capital: *"**if one cannot remain invested for at least 10-years, the capital may not be suitable for investing at all.**"*

This is not a restriction on your liquidity; funds can always be withdrawn if circumstances change. Rather, it is a rule of Original Intent. It means money should only enter an investment vehicle if the initial plan allows it to remain untouched for a full decade.
The specifics of strategy are secondary to the prerequisite of time.
Before solving for how to invest, this rule determines if one should be investing at all.

THE INTERNAL COMPASS

Time simplifies decisions before it multiplies outcomes.

With a timeline clearly defined, attention can move beyond the internal discipline of the investor to the external factors that influence what is ultimately retained.
These forces operate quietly but significantly over long periods, acting as the invisible friction or fuel for your capital.

CHAPTER 3: THE HIDDEN FORCES THAT SHAPE REAL RETURNS

Market returns are often discussed in isolation. What ultimately matters, however, is not what investments earn, but what investors keep.
Between the numbers on a statement and the money available to spend, there are several forces that quietly shape the final result.
These factors rarely attract attention when the market is rising, yet over many years, their combined effect can significantly change your path.
This chapter focuses on those influences, not to discourage the reader, but to provide a clear view of the difference between *"paper profits"* and *"the actual wealth"* that reaches your pocket. It is the difference between the theory of growth and the reality of ownership.

THE PERFORMANCE ILLUSION

Headline returns often ignore the costs and frictions that accompany long-term investing.
Two investors earning the same market return can experience very different outcomes depending on how these hidden forces are managed.
Over long periods, small differences compound into meaningful gaps.
Understanding these factors early prevents unrealistic expectations later.

Factor 1 | Inflation: The Invisible Erosion

Inflation is the quiet reduction of what your money can actually do.
It doesn't announce itself with a crash; it simply makes the world more expensive while your "number" stays the same.
If your investment grows but the cost of your life grows faster, you are not gaining ground- you are retreating.
Over decades, this "silent tide" can wash away the value of a fortune even if the account balance looks healthy.
The goal isn't just to have more money; it is to maintain the strength of your money.

Factor 2 | Taxation: The Structural Reduction

Taxation is not a market event; it is a structural certainty.

While inflation erodes value silently, taxation reduces the portion of returns that actually remain yours.

Two investors earning identical market returns can experience very different outcomes depending on how gains are taxed.

The difference is rarely a skill- it is the structure.

Every time a tax is triggered, capital is removed from the system, abruptly interrupting the momentum of compounding.

A gain that looks impressive on a statement can feel underwhelming once the obligation is settled.

Real progress is measured by post-tax results. The goal is not just to earn, but to ensure your capital remains investable.

Factor 3 | Costs and Fees: The Constant Friction

Every investment carries friction. Management fees, transaction charges, and advisory costs may seem insignificant in isolation, but time magnifies their presence.

Unlike market risk, which fluctuates, costs are predictable and persistent. Even a small, recurring expense reduces the base on which future returns compound. Over long horizons, this "negative compounding" quietly widens the gap between the market's performance and your actual result. The challenge is not complexity, it is attention. Costs that are ignored do not disappear; they accumulate.

In long-term investing, controlling costs is often more reliable than attempting to improve performance.

Factor 4 | Timing: The Behavioral Leak

Markets move in cycles, but investor behavior often moves in reactions. While market movements are out of your control, the timing of your entry and exit is not, and, it is here that the most significant wealth is often lost. Exiting during uncertainty converts temporary volatility into permanent loss. Conversely, waiting for "the right time" to re-enter usually means missing the most productive recovery phases.

These errors are rarely visible on a monthly statement, but they represent a massive "hidden cost" to your long-term success.
Time in the market consistently outweighs the precision of entry.

Factor 5 | Psychological Gap: The Human Element
The most underestimated force in investing is our own nature. Fear, impatience, and the need for certainty often influence decisions more than analysis ever could.
Markets test discipline before they reward patience. Those who react emotionally tend to interrupt compounding at the very moments it is most needed. This gap rarely feels like a mistake; it often feels like protection, until the long-term impact becomes visible.
Discipline is not about ignoring risk; it is about resisting unnecessary action.

Factor 6 | Opportunity Cost: The Hidden Comparison
Capital that remains idle or trapped in low-growth environments loses momentum relative to alternatives. This loss is rarely noticed because it does not appear as a decline, but only as a missed possibility.
Safety without growth carries its own cost over time. Preserving value without allowing it to progress can quietly delay long-term objectives. Opportunity cost is cumulative, not immediate; its impact becomes clear only when time has already passed.
The greatest risk is not just losing money, but missing the growth required to reach your destination.

Factor 7 | Liquidity Constraints: The Forced Exit Risk
Even strong investments can fail if the capital is required at the wrong moment. Liquidity constraints force decisions that strategy alone cannot prevent. When long-term assets are accessed prematurely, timing becomes irrelevant, where outcomes are dictated by necessity rather than a choice. Matching your investment horizon with your liquidity needs is not a technical preference; it is a structural requirement.
Wealth is only as strong as your ability to leave it untouched.

UNDERSTANDING LONG-TERM OUTCOMES

Real returns are not defined by markets alone. They are shaped by inflation, taxation, costs, timing, behavior, and the structural decisions made along the way.

What survives these forces determines true progress. Understanding them early, does not eliminate uncertainty- it replaces unrealistic expectations with informed patience.

With these realities acknowledged, we can now explore how time itself becomes the most powerful ally in building lasting wealth.

From Headline Return to Real Outcome

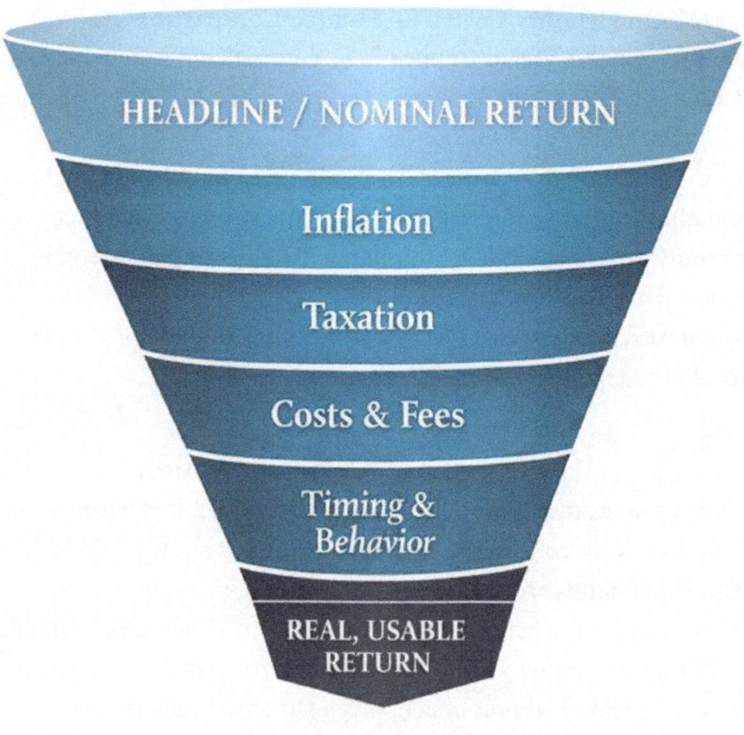

CHAPTER 4: THE 10-YEAR HORIZON- THE DISCIPLINE TEST

The first decade of investing is not designed to reward you.
It is designed to test you.
Most people enter the market with a destination in mind- an amount, a return, or a target date. Very few enter with a commitment to time.
This difference explains why many portfolios begin with optimism but end in disappointment.
The 10-year horizon is not where wealth is created.
It is where investors are separated from spectators.

WHY TIME, NOT PRICE, DEFINES INVESTING

A common mindset dominates modern investing:
"I will exit when I reach my profit." This approach feels logical, but it quietly converts investing into speculation.
Price-based exits are reactive as they respond to emotion, headlines, and short-term validation while Time-based commitment works differently.
When you decide in advance that capital will remain invested for at least a decade, you remove the need to constantly judge outcomes and replace prediction with endurance.
Investing begins when you stop asking, "Is this working right now?" and start asking, "Does this deserve time?"

THE FIRST DECADE IS ABOUT SURVIVAL

The market does not reward patience immediately.

In the first 10-years, one will experience:

- Extended periods of underperformance
- Sharp draw-downs that challenge conviction
- Long stretches where effort feels unrewarded

What most people interpret as failure during this phase is actually a friction- the cost of participation.

The 10-year horizon absorbs this friction. Shorter timelines magnify it. If capital cannot remain untouched for ten years, it should not be exposed to long-term risk. This is not a judgment, it is a filter.

THE ACOUSTIC SHIFT: MOVING FROM NOISE TO SIGNAL

In the first decade, noise dominates perception. You aren't just fighting the market; you are fighting your own senses:

- News feels urgent (but it's usually distraction)
- Volatility feels personal (but it's just market breathing)
- Temporary losses feel permanent (but it's the price of participation)

Evidence that a strategy actually works- the Signal, takes a full decade to emerge. The 10-year mark is the "Filter Point" where the noise fades and the mathematical truth of your growth becomes visible.

Those who exit, at Year-3 or Year-7, never allow this transition to happen. They are like a homeowner trying to move into a house before the concrete foundation has even set.

THE ILLUSION OF FAILURE

The greatest investing mistakes are emotional, not technical.
Most investors quit during the "boring" middle or a sharp drawdown, unaware they are standing on the doorstep of exponential growth.
The 10-year horizon is your emotional armor; it protects the capital from your impulses when the market feels the hardest.

THE DISCIPLINE RULE

The rule is non-negotiable:
"If you cannot commit to a decade, do not invest a single Rupee."
This is not a guarantee of wealth, but a filter for eligibility.
The first ten years do not exist to make you rich; they exist to prove you can handle the volatility required to become wealthy.
You are paying the entry fee for the right to compound.

TRANSITION FORWARD

Once the discipline of time is established, a new question emerges:
What happens when time is no longer the constraint,
but the advantage?
That answer belongs to the next horizon.

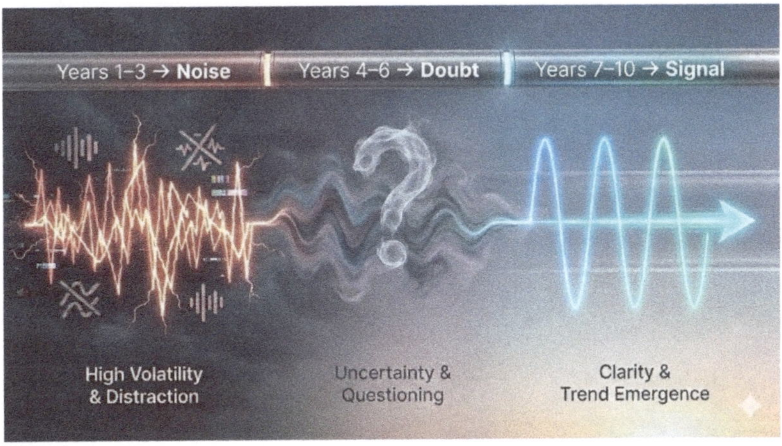

CHAPTER 5: THE 20-YEAR HORIZON- WHEN STRATEGY REPLACES LUCK

If the first decade is about survival, the second is about validation.
"By 10th year, the investor has already done something rare: they stayed."
The next ten years answer a different question, not whether you can endure, but whether what you built deserves endurance.
This is the horizon where randomness begins to lose influence and structure begins to matter.

WHY LUCK FADES OVER TWENTY YEARS

In the short term, outcomes are distorted by timing.
In the long term, outcomes are shaped by process.
Over 20 years:

- Good decisions repeat
- Poor structures expose themselves
- Temporary advantages disappear
- Sustainable ones compound

Luck still exists, but its power diminishes. Strategy gains weight.
This is the point where investing becomes less about hope and more about design.

FROM PARTICIPATION TO PROOF

During the first decade, capital simply needed time. During the second, capital needs direction a stage where patterns emerge.
Allocation decisions begin to matter more than *entry prices.*
This is where investing moves from participation to proof of concept.
You are no longer guessing whether your approach works; you are observing how it behaves.

THE LOGIC OF CONTINUITY

The Trust Principle- True risk is no longer the price you pay today, but the growth you forfeit tomorrow.
The Operator's Edge- While intelligence seeks the "best" move, consistency creates the model that stays with a "good" move, proving that brilliance is only a moment, but consistency is a result.

THE STRUCTURAL THINKING ERA

This is the decade where structure begins to matter. Questions evolve from "Should I stay invested?" to "How should this be arranged?" The answers are no longer philosophical; they are architectural. While execution comes later, the lesson for now is simple:
"a strategy that survives 20 years earns the right to compound."

TRANSITION FORWARD

At 20 years, wealth becomes visible.
At 30, it becomes inevitable.
What changes when time stops testing strategy, and begins to enforce it? That is the domain of the next horizon.

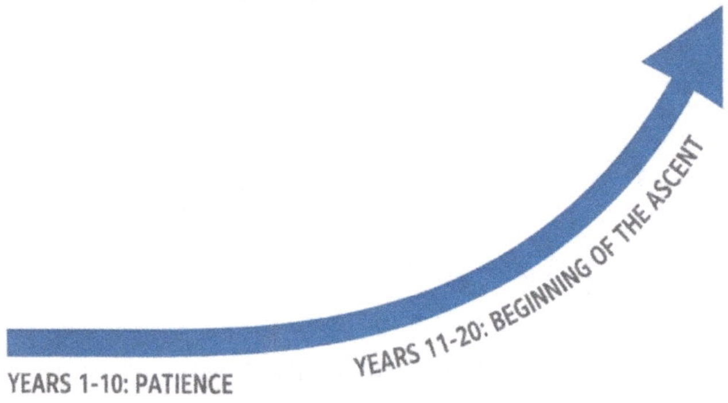

CHAPTER 6: THE 30-YEAR HORIZON- WHEN TIME TAKES CONTROL

Thirty years changes the nature of wealth.
Not gradually, but structurally.
Compounding beyond three decades is no longer about participation or validation. It becomes momentum.
Returns begin to influence returns in visible magnitude.
The growth curve shifts from linear perception to exponential reality.
The investor is no longer building capital. Capital is expanding itself.

THE SHIFT FROM EFFORT TO MOMENTUM

In earlier decades, outcomes respond to behavior and allocation.
At the last one, outcomes respond to accumulated duration.
Earlier consistency becomes embedded leverage.
*The defining feature of this horizon is **acceleration**.*
Not because risk increased⚠️
Not because strategy changed🎯
But because time accumulated⏳

COMPOUNDING IS NOT PROPORTIONAL

Growth in early years appears modest relative to effort while in later stage, it seems disproportionate relative to adjustment.
This asymmetry is the defining characteristic of long-term investing.
The final decade of a 30-year cycle often contributes more than the first fifteen combined.

NOMINAL VS REAL VALUE

Over decades, numbers grow. Balances expand. Statements impress.
The figure becomes larger, sometimes dramatically so.
Yet inflation moves quietly besides it.
It does not shrink the number but what the number can buy.
Thirty years later, "*Nominal Wealth*" may look powerful but
"*Real Wealth*" may tell a different story.
Compounding without purchasing power is only arithmetic.
True wealth is measured in economic strength.

THE REALITY CHECK

Scenario	Nominal Value (On Paper)	Real Value (In Reality)	Outcome
Growth < Inflation	Numbers go up 📈	Purchasing power falls 📉	Silent erosion
Growth = Inflation	Numbers go up 📈	Purchasing power preserved 🛑	No advancement
Growth > Inflation	Numbers go up 📈	Purchasing power expands 🚀	True wealth

THE DISCIPLINE OF REAL GROWTH

Markets reward returns. Time rewards discipline.
But only purchasing power builds freedom.
Nominal size is visibility. Real value is capability.
The investor who understands this difference, stops chasing larger numbers and starts protecting economic power.

THE FRAGILITY OF SUCCESS

Wealth at 30 years is powerful, but not invulnerable.

The risks shift from volatility to:

- Concentration
- Overconfidence
- Structural imbalance
- Tax inefficiency

The more wealth compounds, the more precision matters.

Small structural errors now carry large consequences.

THE VERTICAL PHASE

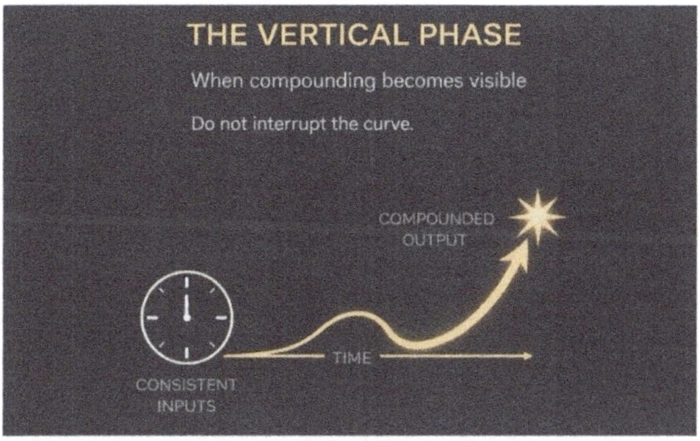

Compounding looks slow… until it is not.

The steepest gains arrive at the end of the curve.

Most people abandon the process in the flat years.

The vertical phase belongs only to those who did not interrupt it.

It is about ensuring permanence.

THE PRESERVATION SHIFT

After thirty years, wealth no longer needs aggressive expansion.

It needs protection.

The objective changes from acceleration to sustainability.

This phase is not about building more.

It is about ensuring permanence.

CHAPTER 7: ENDURANCE POWER

Compounding is simple in theory 📖
It is difficult in duration ⏳
The early years are energetic ⚡
The later years are rewarding 🏆
The middle years are quiet 🤫
This is where most investors stop 🛑
Not because the strategy failed 🎯
Because patience did ⏳🥀

THE HIDDEN EQUATION

<u>Compounding survives on three forces:</u>

Time × Discipline × Emotional Stability

Time passes automatically.
Discipline does not.
Stability is rare.
Remove one, and the curve never turns vertical.

THE DANGEROUS MIDDLE

Years **(1–3)** feel *active*.
Years **(7–10)** feel *powerful*.
Years **(4–6)** feel *ordinary*.

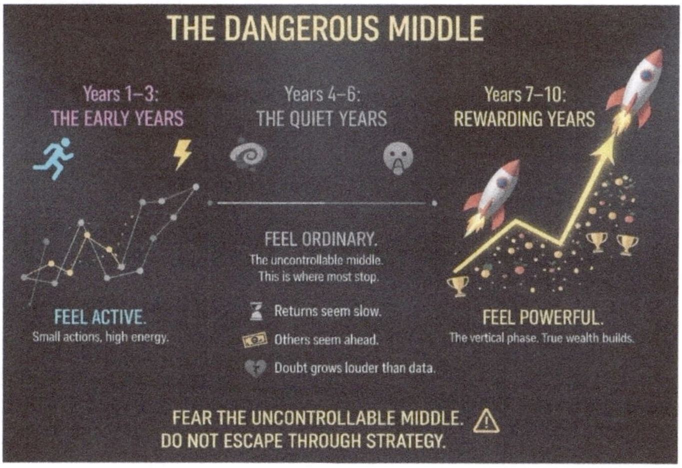

THE STRUCTURAL TRUTH

Most investors do not fail in the beginning. They fail in the middle.
Not because returns disappear, but because excitement does.
The dangerous years are not the worst-performing ones but the most ordinary ones.

Nothing feels exceptional.
Progress continues, just not fast enough to satisfy impatience.
So strategies are changed. Risk is increased. Plans are abandoned.
Not due to data but discomfort.
Compounding is interrupted by reaction rather than the volatility.

The market tests performance.
Time tests endurance.

Only one of those determines who reaches the vertical phase.

The greatest risk is not loss.

It is leaving too soon.

CHAPTER 8: THE COMMITMENT AGAINST INTERRUPTION

Compounding does not fail.
It gets interrupted.
Not by markets, but shortened commitment.

THE REAL RISK

The greatest threat to long-term wealth is not volatility.
It is changing your time horizon mid-journey.
"Starting with a 20-year mindset…reacting with a 2-year emotion."
That gap destroys outcomes.

THE UNSPOKEN SOLUTION

Before investing, make sure to follow these rules:
For the next 10-years, "I will not evaluate success annually."
For the next 20-years, "I will not abandon strategy due to boredom."
For the next 30-years, "I will let compounding finish its work."
This is not optimism. It is a structural patience.

THE 10–20–30 HORIZON

10-Years : Filters noise
20-Years : Makes compounding visible
30-Years : Makes wealth meaningful
Anything shorter invites interruption
Anything longer builds permanence

PSYCHOLOGICAL SHIFT

Stop asking:
"What if the market falls?"
Start asking:
"Am I committed long enough?"
Because Downturns are temporary while Interruption is permanent.

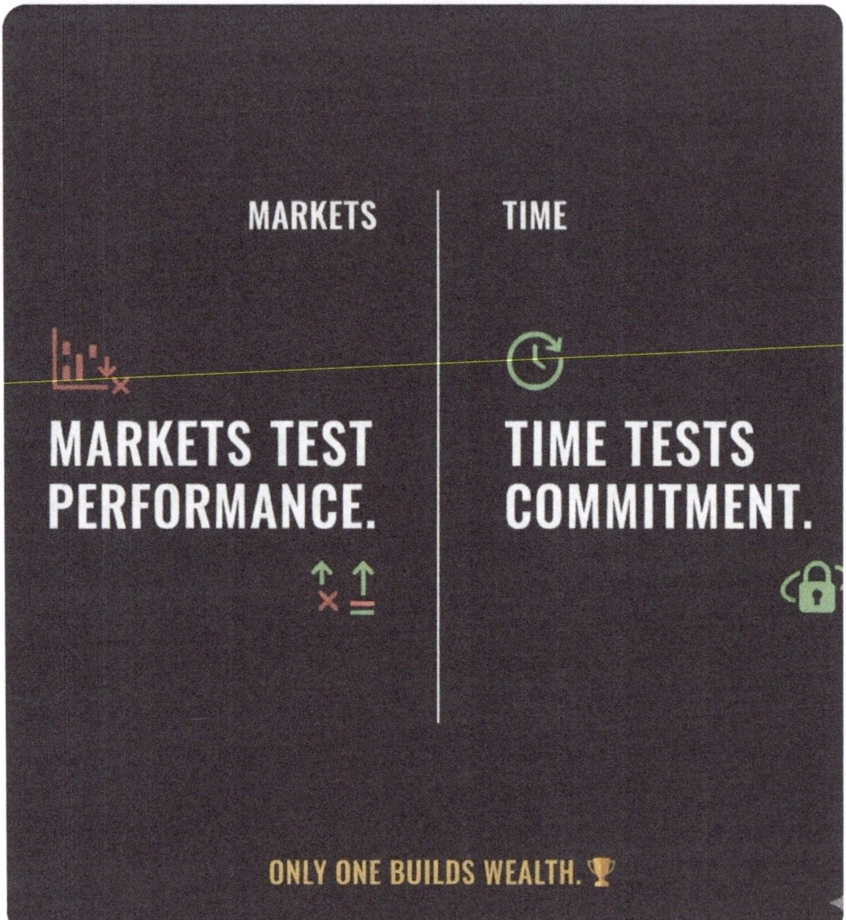
MARKETS
TIME
MARKETS TEST PERFORMANCE.
TIME TESTS COMMITMENT.
ONLY ONE BUILDS WEALTH.

CHAPTER 9: ASSET-WISE TIME HORIZON

THE STRUCTURAL HOLDING RULE

Commitment without structure is fragile. Not every asset deserves the same patience. Time horizon must match asset nature.
When they mismatch, wealth gets interrupted.

THE CORE PRINCIPLE

Short-term money should not enter long-term assets.
Long-term assets should not be judged short-term.
Most investing mistakes are not about selection.
They are about timeline confusion.

1. **EQUITIES-** *TIME DEMANDS PATIENCE*
   ***Minimum Holding Horizon*:** 10-Years
   ***Ideal Horizon*:** 20–30 Years

- Equities are volatile in the short term but are transformative in the long term.
- Three years in equities is speculation while Thirty years is ownership.

2. **DEBT / FIXED INCOME-** *STABILITY WINDOW*
   ***Holding Horizon*:** 3–10 Years
   Debt instruments exist to:

- Reduce volatility
- Provide predictable returns
- Offer capital stability

They are not growth engines but structural stabilizers.

3. **CASH-** *IMMEDIATE LIQUIDITY*
   Holding Horizon: 0–2 Years

- Cash has one job which is to prevent forced selling.
- Emergency needs, short-term goals, and psychological comfort belong here.

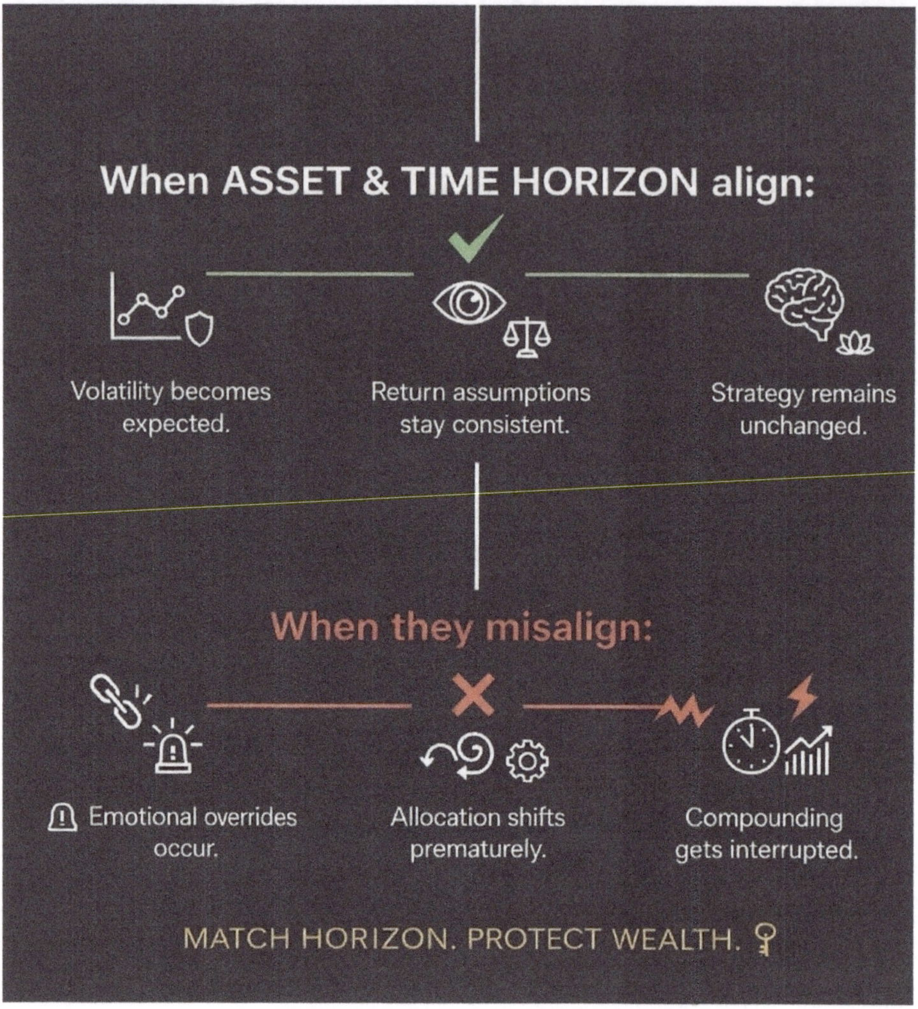

Time horizon is a design decision, not a market prediction.

CHAPTER 10: ONE PRINCIPLE, TWO PATHS

Same economy
Same inflation
Same tax
Same return
Different method.

EXAMPLE ILLUSTRATION- LUMP SUM VS SIP UNDER SAME CONDITIONS

Assumptions:

Return assumption represents total return, including reinvested dividends.

Initial Lump Sum: ₹10,00,000
Monthly SIP: ₹20,000
Return: 12% per year
Inflation: 6% per year
Tax: 12.5% LTCG
Period: 30 years

Time Horizon	Lump Sum Nominal Value	Lump Sum Real Value	SIP Nominal Value	SIP Real Value
10 years	₹31 lakh	₹16 lakh	₹46 lakh	₹24 lakh
20 years	₹96 lakh	₹27 lakh	₹2.0 crore	₹62 lakh
30 years	₹3.0 crore	₹57 lakh	₹7.0 crore	₹1.52 crore

(Values rounded for clarity. Calculations based on stated assumptions.)

Nominal value shows the number. Real value shows its purchasing power.

UNDERSTANDING THE ILLUSTRATION

- The illustration compares two forms of investing under identical economic conditions.
- It shows how time, inflation, and taxation influence the final purchasing power of wealth.
- While the nominal value appears large over long periods, the real value reflects its true economic strength.
- Both approaches benefit from time. Their difference lies in how capital is deployed and sustained.

DISCLAIMER

This illustration is provided for educational purposes only.

It is based on assumed rates of return, inflation, and taxation applicable in India at the time of writing, which may change in the future.

Actual future returns, inflation, tax policies, and market conditions may vary significantly.

This example does not represent any guaranteed outcome or specific investment recommendation.

Individual results will differ based on personal investment decisions and economic conditions.

TIME CHANGES NUMBERS.
INFLATION DEFINES THEIR MEANING.

CHAPTER 11: THE EXECUTOR'S BLUEPRINT

WHERE WEALTH BECOMES ENDURING

Wealth is not complete when it is built.
It is complete when it can sustain life without interrupting its own future.
Building wealth requires discipline.
Preserving wealth requires structure.
Using wealth requires restraint.

THE THREE PHASES OF WEALTH

Every long-term portfolio passes through three structural phases.
These phases are not defined by age. They are defined by time invested.

The First Decade- *Foundation*

In the early years, compounding is still forming.
Progress appears slow.
The base is fragile.
This phase is not designed for withdrawal.
It is designed for protection.
Time must be allowed to establish the structure.
Interruptions here carry consequences that are invisible immediately, but significant later.

The Second Decade- *Expansion*

In the second phase, the effect of compounding becomes visible.
Growth begins accelerating.
The portfolio starts contributing more than the original investment.
This phase introduces flexibility.
Limited, planned withdrawal becomes possible if required.
But the structure must remain intact.
Growth must continue.

The Third Decade- *Endurance*

In the final phase, the system matures.

Time has already done its most important work.

Wealth begins serving its purpose.

This phase allows wealth to support life.

Income

Freedom

Security.

Without ending its continuity.

THE DUAL-ACCOUNT STRUCTURE

The two-account framework exists for this moment.

Each account has a role.

Account A exists to be used.

- It provides liquidity when required.
- Over long periods, it can support important life needs without disturbing the entire system.

Account B exists to remain uninterrupted.

- It continues compounding across decades.
- It is not designed for early use.
- It is designed for endurance.

This separation protects long-term compounding from short-term requirements.

THE STRUCTURAL WITHDRAWAL APPROACH

Wealth survives longest when withdrawal and compounding are not forced to compete.

When one account supports life, the other continues building the future.

This ensures continuity, not depletion.

STRUCTURAL ROLE ACROSS TIME

	Account A Role	Account B Role
First Decade	Protection and growth	Continuous compounding
Second Decade	Supports selected needs if required	Remains uninterrupted
Third Decade	Provides stability and income support	Continues as long-term reserve

THE LAW OF UNINTERRUPTED ENDURANCE

"Volatility is temporary, but interruption is permanent."

While the world fears the temporary noise of the market, the real risk to your wealth has always been the breaking of the chain.

Inflation is gradual and taxation is structural, but only interruption is fatal.

True wealth is not defined by its size, but by its ability to endure.

By building a structure that protects your capital from your own impulses, you move from the stress of speculation to the certainty of time.

Wealth is the reward for the discipline of staying out of Time's way while it completes its work.

Time is the builder.

Structure is the protector.

Discipline is the executor.

Wealth is the result.

THE EPILOGUE: A PROMISE TO TIME

This book was never a prediction of the future; it was a blueprint for your present. Wealth is rarely destroyed by market declines.
It is destroyed by the decision to stop. Compounding doesn't ask for your brilliance, your timing, or your perfection. It only asks for your continuity.

There will be years where discipline feels like a burden and periods where nothing appears to happen. There will be moments where quitting feels
like the only reasonable choice. But compounding hides its strength in the beginning; it only reveals its power at the end.

This work exists to help you stay long enough to witness the math.
The goal is not to do more, but to interrupt less.

What stays invested, stays in motion.
And what stays in motion, time builds.

BEYOND THE HORIZON

ABOUT THE AUTHOR

"I am an architect by profession and an observer of how time shapes outcomes.

In design, I learned that true structural integrity is not born of complexity, but of alignment, patience, and continuity. Over the years, I have come to realize that these same principles govern the accumulation of wealth. This book is the blueprint of that realization.

I am not a registered financial advisor. Instead, I use these pages to translate my observations into a creative framework, fueled by personal experience and long-term study. This work—my first—is less a rigid strategy and more a philosophy. It treats time not as a volatile variable, but as the master builder.

For those who connect with these pages, my goal is simple: to help you hold your ground until time reveals the masterpiece."

ABOUT THE AUTHOR

BUILT BY TIME,
SECURED BY STRUCTURE,
AND LEFT UNINTERRUPTED.

BUILT BY TIME was written, designed, and independently published by Piyush Mittal.

Printed and bound in India.

First edition.

THE 10-YEAR RULE

If you cannot
stay invested for
10-Years,
you should
question
why you own
it at all.

Markets move everyday.

Wealth

moves over

decades.

TIME makes you wise & wealthy.

TIME HORIZON

Every investment decision begins with one question-

How long can you stay patient?

Before choosing investments,

firstly decide-

Are you truly an investor, or

someone simply reacting to markets?

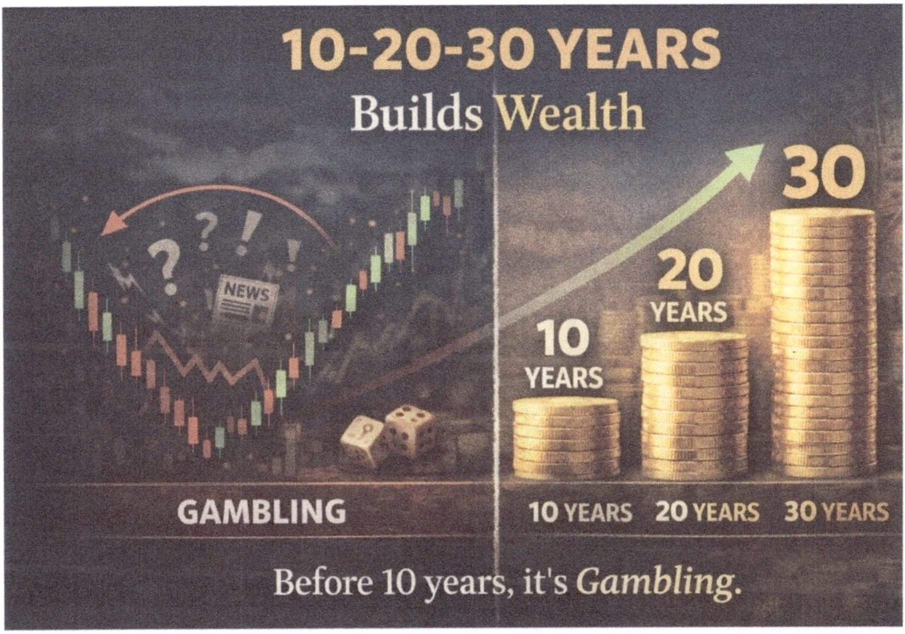

TIME reveals your mindset.

Investors think in **DECADES**.

Long-term investing

is not something you own

and forget.

It is something you **believe in**

everyday.

Most wealth is not created by

utilizing skill...

But by staying

long enough

patiently.

SHORT HORIZONS create stress.

LONG HORIZONS create clarity.

WHAT IS YOUR
TIME HORIZON?
Short-Term
Long-Term
NOISE OR WEALTH?

STRUCTURE

Time is the only
builder that works at
the pace required for
strong foundations.

Interrupt the
process, and
the structure
collapses.

CHOOSE WISELY.

TIME FILTERS
NOISE
NEWS
LOSS

Measure progress not in days.

Measure it in ***decades.***

COMPOUNDING
IS INVISIBLE
UNTIL IT BECOMES OBVIOUS
0 YEARS → 5 YEARS → 10 YEARS → 30 YEARS

BUILT BY TIME PRINCIPLES

1. The 10-Year Rule

2. Time Horizon Determines Outcomes

3. Compounding Needs Silence

4. Volatility Is Not Risk

5. Structure Protects Wealth

6. Long Horizons Create Clarity

7. Patience Is The Multiplier

8. Wealth Is Built, Not Found

REFLECTION

*What is **my time horizon**?*

BUILT BY TIME

Wealth

built

slowly

lasts

the

longest.

9 789357 778374

Printed at Repro India Ltd.